Selecte

SONATINAS

MW01250793

Volume I

Early Intermediate to Intermediate Piano Solos

Compiled and Edited by Dale Tucker

Editor: Dale Tucker
Art Design: Joann Carrera
Artwork Reproduced on Cover: *The Dance* (detail) by Jean Antoine Watteau

CONTENTS

COMPOSER BIOGRAPHIES

Ludwig van Beethoven was born December 16, 1770, in Bonn, Germany. His family was musical and he received musical training from an early age. Beethoven was thirteen when his first compositions were published. Soon after, he became a church organist, continued to study and compose, and gained the respect of colleagues and wealthy patrons. Beethoven moved to Vienna, Austria, in 1792 and remained there until his death March 26, 1827. In Vienna he studied with Haydn, Salieri, and others. He went on to compose for piano, voice, choir, chamber ensembles, and orchestra. He is perhaps best known for his famous Ninth Symphony, which combines the forces of a large orchestra and chorus.

Albert Biehl was born in Germany in 1835 and died in 1899. He had a reputation as a fine music teacher.

Muzio Clementi was born January 23, 1752, in Rome, Italy. His family enjoyed music but played no instruments. Young Clementi first studied piano and organ with his local church choirmaster and then moved on to include voice and composition lessons. By the age of fourteen, he was performing concerts. He moved soon thereafter to England to continue his musical training and later became a famed concert pianist and conductor. Unlike many composers of the period, Clementi became wealthy from teaching, performing, and composing. Clementi died at his home in Euesham, England, March 10, 1832, after a brief illness. His funeral was held at Westminster Abbey in London to a capacity crowd of mourners.

Johann Ladislav Dussek was born February 12, 1760, in Čáslav, Bohemia, and began studying piano at the age of five and organ at the age of nine. He had a beautiful voice as a child and became a chorister at the Menorite church in Iglau. He continued to study at the Jesuit College and Prague University. After graduation, he did further study with C. P. E. Bach. He performed piano concerts across Europe, often playing before royalty and such notables as Marie Antoinette and Napoleon. During the French Revolution, he fled to England, where he continued to perform and teach, and then fled from creditors in England back to Germany after squandering much of his earnings. Years of obesity and drinking led to poor health and ultimately Dussek's death March 20, 1812, in Paris.

Friedrich Kuhlau was born September 11, 1786, in Ülzen, Germany. As a child he lost sight in one eye following an accident. During his recovery period, he began to study piano. His father was leader of a military band, so they moved often. One such move took him to Hamburg, where he continued study of theory and composition. There he also became renowned as a teacher. In 1810 Kuhlau moved to Copenhagen, Denmark, to avoid serving in Napoleon's army, and there developed a reputation as a fine pianist and composer. He was appointed court musician in 1813 and performed concerts across Europe, but he did not enjoy a lavish lifestyle. He died in Copenhagen March 12, 1832, leaving behind a musical legacy of works for piano, solo voice, instrumental solos and ensembles, and stage works.

SONATINA IN C MAJOR

Opus 57, No. 1

ALBERT BIEHL

Allegro moderato

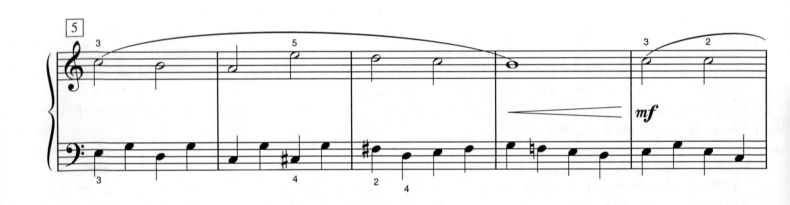

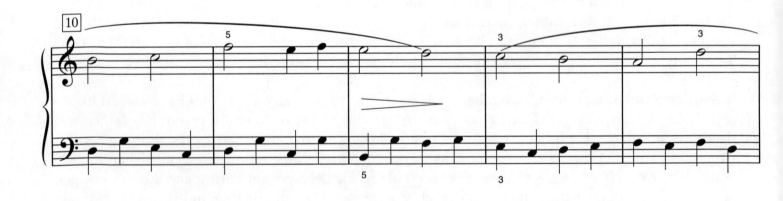

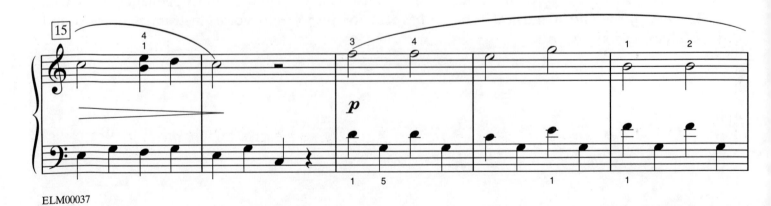

6

Allegro grazioso

SONATINA IN C MAJOR

Opus 36, No. 1

MUZIO CLEMENTI

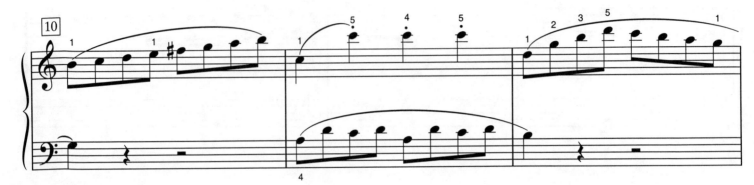

ELM00037

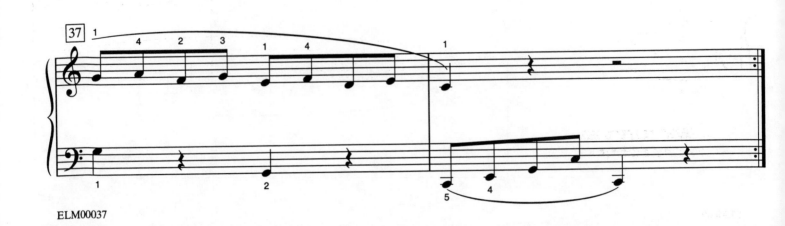

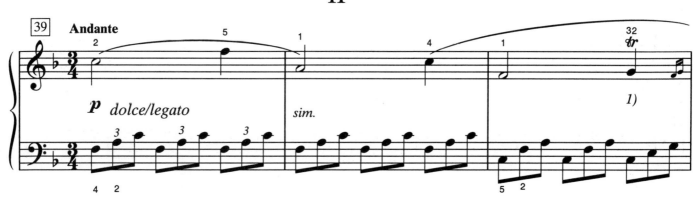

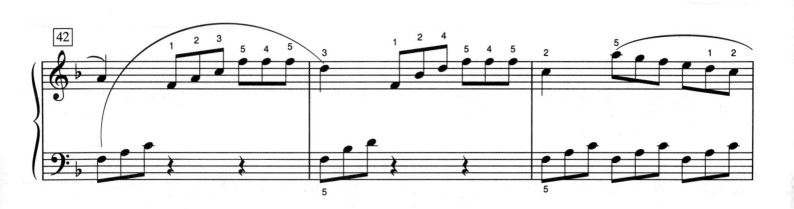

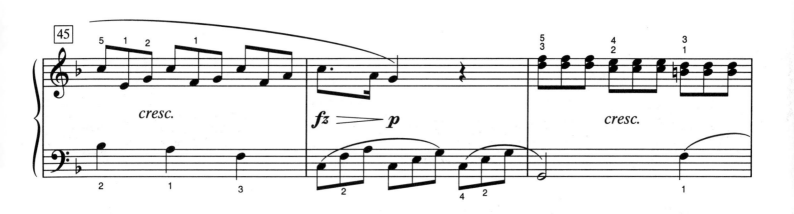

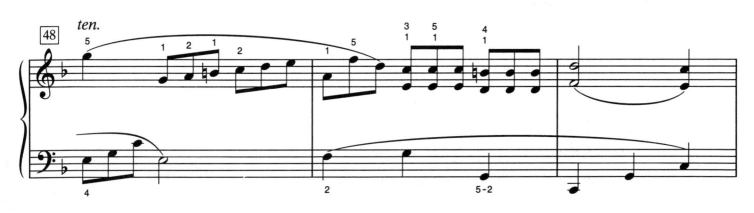

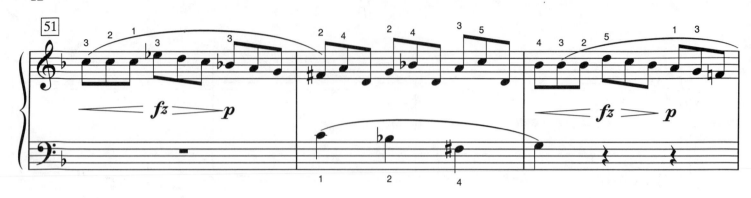

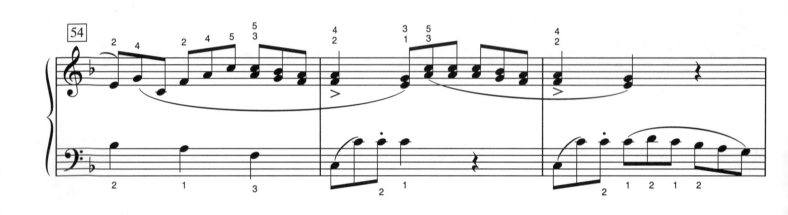

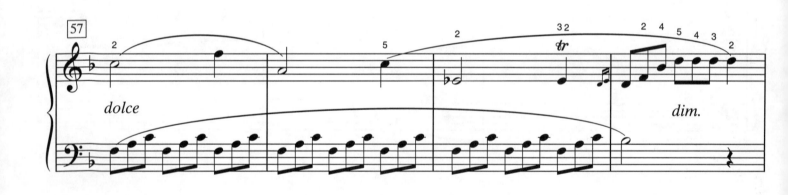

III

14

ELM00037

SONATINA IN C MAJOR

Opus 55, No. 1

FRIEDRICH KUHLAU

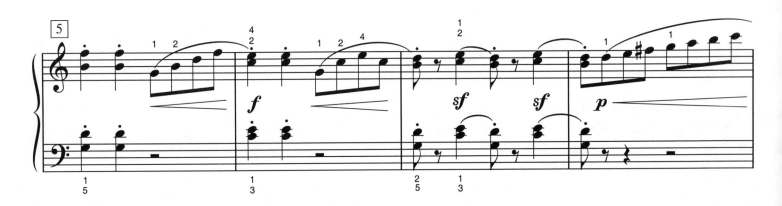

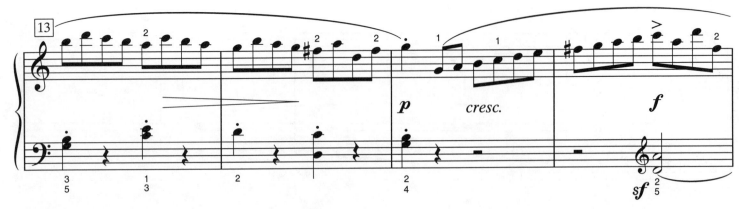

20

ELM00037

SONATINA IN F MAJOR
Opus 38, No. 3

MUZIO CLEMENTI

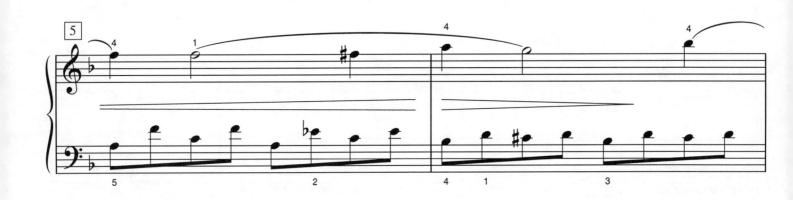

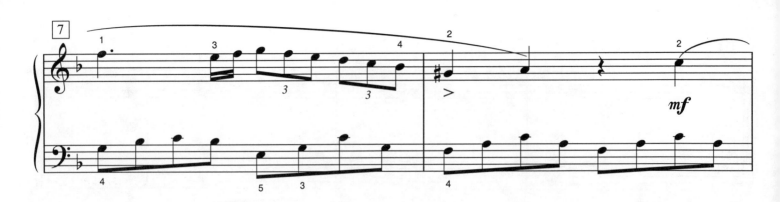

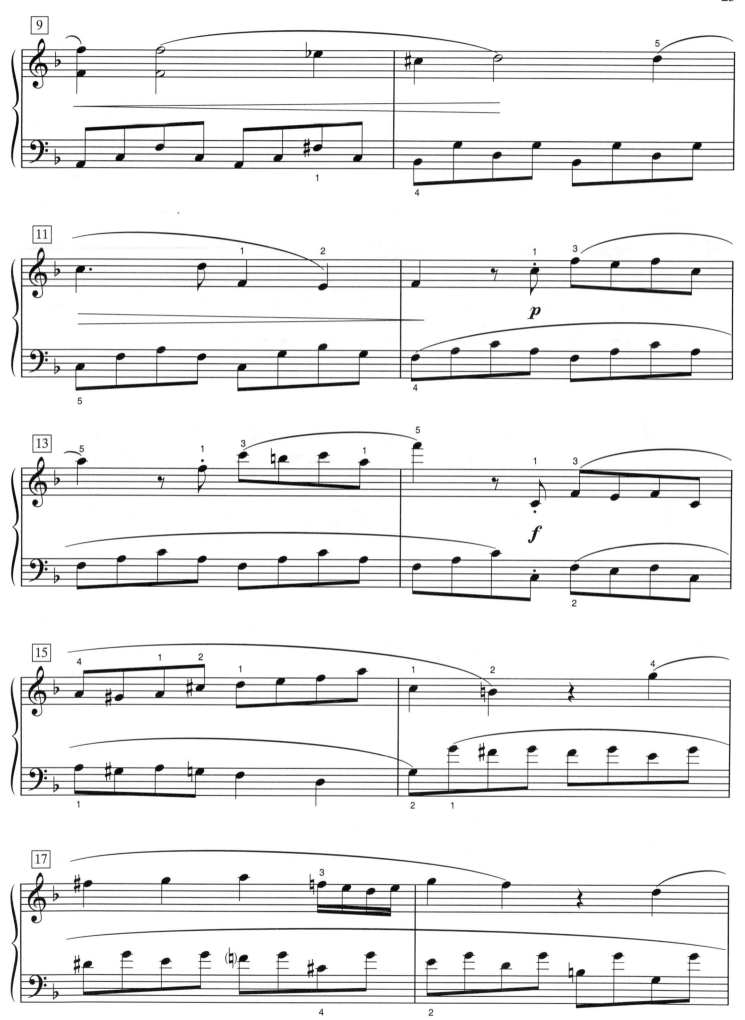

30

SONATINA IN G MAJOR

LUDWIG VAN BEETHOVEN

Moderato

32

ELM00037

Romanze

34

SONATINA IN F MAJOR

LUDWIG VAN BEETHOVEN

Allegro assai

36

ELM00037

38

ELM00037

Rondo

40

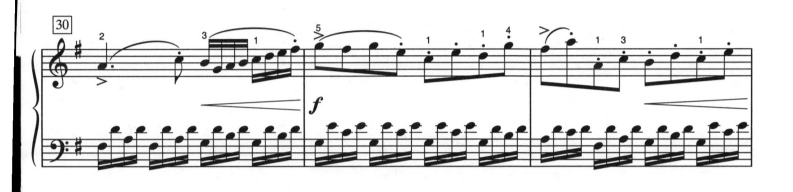

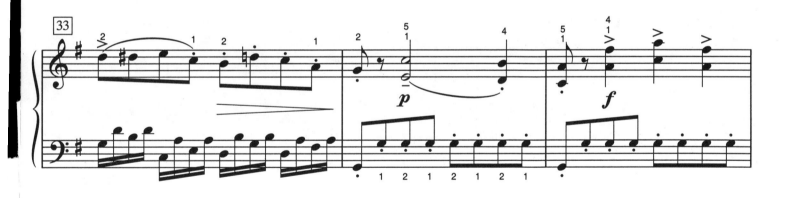

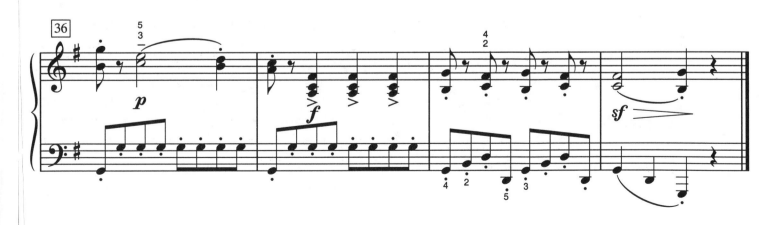

ELM00037

Rondo

Allegretto (Tempo di Minuetto)

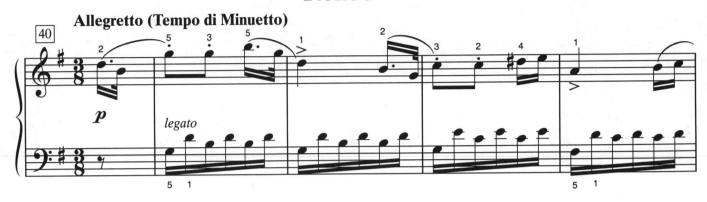

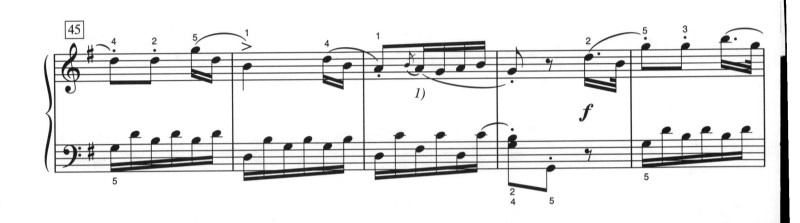

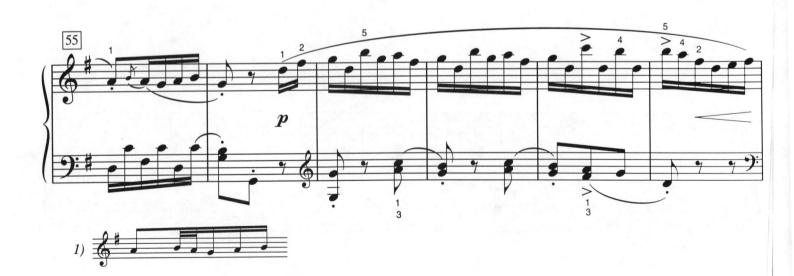

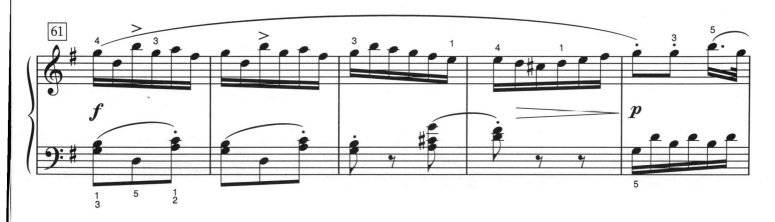

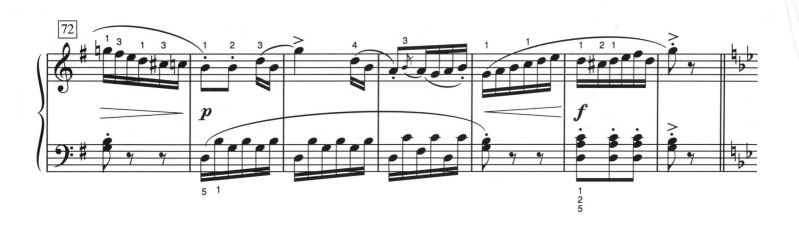

Minore

46

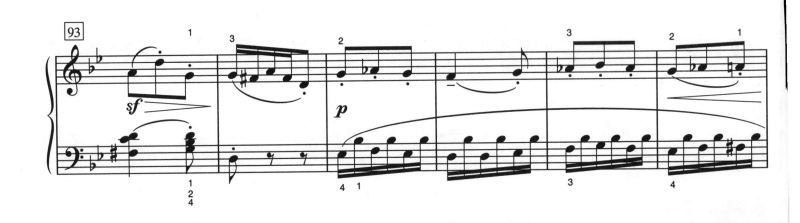

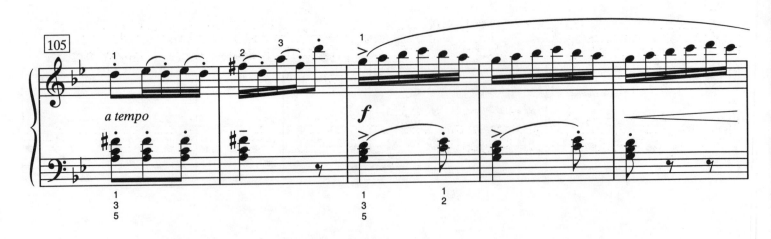

ELM00037

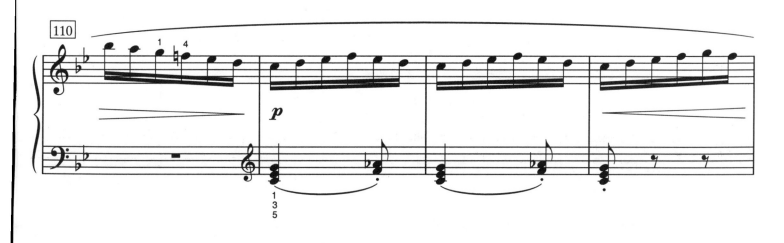

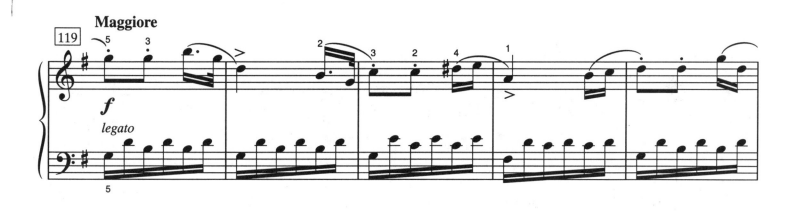

SONATINA IN G MAJOR
Opus 20, No. 1

JOHANN LADISLAV DUSSEK

Allegro non tanto

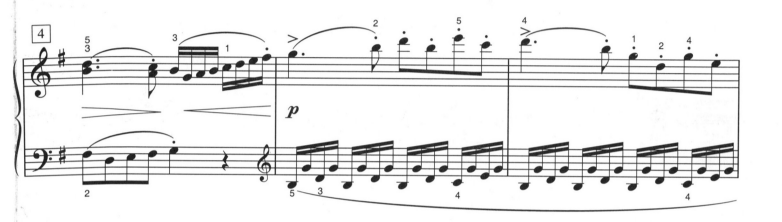

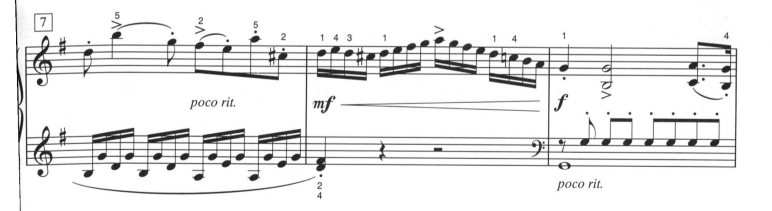

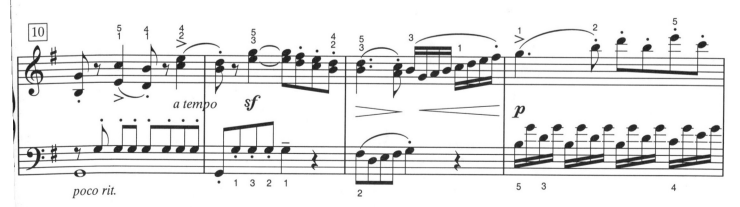

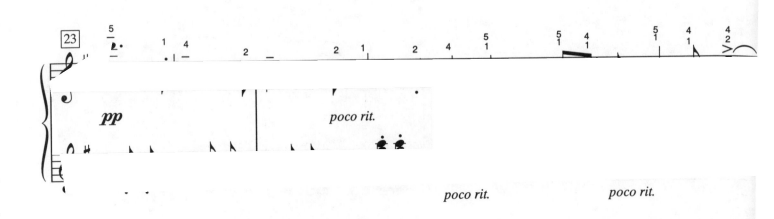